DRAWING WAR

I0139921

Brett Neveu

BROADWAY PLAY PUBLISHING INC
New York
www.broadwayplaypublishing.com
info@broadwayplaypublishing.com

DRAWING WAR
© Copyright 2007 Brett Neveu

Cover art by Rich Sparks
First printing: September 2007
I S B N: 978-0-88145-350-8
Book design: Marie Donovan
Word processing: Microsoft Word
Typographic controls: Ventura Publisher
Typeface: Palatino
Printed and bound in the U S A

DRAWING WAR was first presented by Chicago
Dramatists from 15 March-22 April 2001. The cast
and creative contributors were:

MR BRAUN .... Robert W Behr
CHAD UDELHOVEN .... Justin Cholewa
GRANDMA FANDER .... Kate Winters
JEFF BRAUN .... Phillip Dawkins
MRS BRAUN .... Suellen Burton

Director .... Russ Tutterow
Set design .... Ann Davis
Lighting design .... Jeff Pines
Costume design .... Michelle Lynette Bush
Sound design .... Chris J Johnson
Stage management .... Barbara Walk

SPECIAL THANKS

Ed Sobel, Ann Filmer, Ian Morgan, Russ Tutterow, Chicago Dramatists, AROT, Jonathan Lomma, and Chicago storefront theater.

CHARACTERS & SETTING

CHAD UDELHOVEN, *male, thirteen*
MR BRAUN, *male, forties*
MRS BRAUN, *female, forties*
JEFF BRAUN, *male, seventeen*
GRANDMA FANDER, *female, seventies*

Time: present

Place:Outside a church
A jail cell
A nursing home
The Braun home
A fast food restaurant
A holding area at a courthouse
A graveyard
The UDELHOVEN *home*
all located in a small, midwestern town

to Kristen and Lia Pearl

ACT ONE

Scene 1

(Lights up. Christmas Eve. MR BRAUN *stands alone. He wears a long, heavy coat.)*

*(*CHAD *enters slowly. He holds an umbrella over his head. He stares at* MR BRAUN *for a few beats.)*

CHAD: Merry Christmas, Mister Braun.

MR BRAUN: Hello, Chad.

CHAD: Merry Christmas.

MR BRAUN: Merry Christmas.

CHAD: It's pretty bad weather.

MR BRAUN: It sure is bad. Maybe it will snow later.

CHAD: It's still pretty slick.

MR BRAUN: How's school?

CHAD: Fine. *(Pause)* My mom and I are just waiting for my dad to come pick us up.

MR BRAUN: I hope it isn't too slick to drive.

CHAD: Me too. *(Pause)* We're going to look at lights on houses after this. If it's not too slick.

MR BRAUN: Let's hope it's not. *(Pause)* Seems strange tomorrow is already Jesus's birthday.

CHAD: Yeah.

MR BRAUN: What did they say about Jesus's birthday in Sunday school?

CHAD: Tonight?

MR BRAUN: Yes.

CHAD: They don't have Sunday school on Christmas Eve.

MR BRAUN: Oh.

CHAD: We just came for service.

MR BRAUN: I don't know why I would have thought they would have had Sunday school tonight. I thought I remembered Matt going to Sunday school on Christmas Eve. Probably not, though.

CHAD: I don't go to Sunday school anymore.

MR BRAUN: You don't?

CHAD: We don't come to church that much.

MR BRAUN: You don't?

CHAD: We stopped going every Sunday.

MR BRAUN: I haven't been in awhile, either.

CHAD: Oh.

MR BRAUN: Things have been a little hectic at home, so it's hard to get out on the weekends. Jeff is visiting Grandma Fander at the nursing home tonight, and we're picking Mrs Braun up at the courthouse tomorrow.

CHAD: Oh.

MR BRAUN: They're letting her out on Christmas.

CHAD: Good.

MR BRAUN: I don't know if they did that on purpose, or it just worked out that way. *(Pause)* It's bad weather for Jesus tonight.

CHAD: Yeah.

MR BRAUN: Well, bye.

CHAD: Bye.

(MR BRAUN *exits.*)

(CHAD *stands alone holding his umbrella.*)

(*Lights fade.*)

Scene 2

(*A nursing home.* JEFF *and* GRANDMA *sit at a round, folding table.* GRANDMA *smiles blankly and has dirty teeth.* GRANDMA *smoothes out the placemat in front of her. Both* JEFF *and* GRANDMA *have a piece of peppermint pie in front of them. There is a Christmas present on the table.*)

GRANDMA: It was cold. Cold in the. Shucka shucka shucka shucka shucka shucka...

JEFF: Uh-huh.

GRANDMA: She wasn't going to tell me, she wasn't going to tell me, she was leaving—

JEFF: Do you want some pie, grandma?

(GRANDMA *smiles and looks at* JEFF. JEFF *puts a fork in* GRANDMA*'s hand.*)

(JEFF *and* GRANDMA *eat the peppermint pie.* GRANDMA *eats big pieces of her pie fast, while* JEFF *stops eating after his first bite.*)

JEFF: Eew. Peppermint pie.

(GRANDMA *continues to eat her peppermint pie.*)

(GRANDMA *finishes her pie.*)

JEFF: It's freezing rain outside. (*Long pause*) Do you want to open your Christmas present?

(JEFF *tries to hand the present to* GRANDMA.)

GRANDMA: No, no, no, no.

(GRANDMA *attempts to smooth out the paper on the present.*)

JEFF: Here. I'll start it.

(JEFF *rips a little bit of the paper, then puts* GRANDMA's *hand on the package.* GRANDMA *attempts to smooth the paper back down.* JEFF *rips more of the paper.* GRANDMA *tries to smooth.* JEFF *rips.* GRANDMA *smoothes.*)

(JEFF *tears off all of the paper.*)

JEFF: I'll open the box. (*He takes the present out of the box, which is wrapped in tissue paper. Removing the tissue paper, he reveals a wind up, twirling, mirrored circle topped by a mirror covered angel.*) What the hell is this? Do you like this?

GRANDMA: I don't like it.

JEFF: This can't go in your room.

GRANDMA: You're going to take, yes, shucka, shucka, shucka (*Some clicking sounds*)

(JEFF *winds up the music box.*)

JEFF: *Memory*? It plays *Memory* from *Cats*?

GRANDMA: Oh yes, I like it.

JEFF: Shit. Merry Christmas, Grandma.

(GRANDMA *smoothes out both placemats. She piles them on top of each other, then begins to eat* JEFF's *peppermint pie.*)

(*Lights fade.*)

Scene 3

(MRS BRAUN *sits alone in her jail cell.*)

MRS BRAUN: There was this house that my family used to live in, in New Mexico. This house had been nearly abandoned, but we didn't have any money, so we rented it and fixed it up a little. It had a sunken tub in the back. The house had previously been owned by a Korean couple that had just moved to the United States. They had gotten married right when they came to America, and they were happy. I think there might have been something about the woman's family not approving of the marriage. I'm not sure, I can't remember. Anyhow, the young man was then drafted in the war and the woman was left alone. He was then killed in battle. The young woman was so upset by the news of his death that she went to the kitchen of this house and took a butcher knife out of a drawer and killed herself. When we lived there, my family heard strange noises all of the time. Sometimes late at night, you could hear the drawers in the kitchen opening and the silverware rattling around. You could hear footsteps walking in the upstairs hall. There was a room in the house that was always kept locked, that had the dead young woman's things in it. The door to this room would open and shut by itself. Objects would move around in the house—they would change places. One night, when I was twelve, I was sleeping and something woke me. I looked toward the doorway of my room, and a white figure stood floating above the floor. I watched it for a moment, then I pulled the covers over my face and froze. I prayed to God to make it go away. I prayed for what seemed like hours. I must have fallen asleep, because when I woke up, it was morning. Our family didn't stay in the house much longer. My mother felt the woman's presence once, but she never saw her.

(Lights fade.)

Scene 4

(Christmas music. Christmas morning. Opened boxes and ripped wrapping paper litter the floor. JEFF wears a robe and sits in a large, comfortable chair. He has a sweatshirt draped over him as if see how it will look on. MR BRAUN sits in an opposite chair, smiling at JEFF. A few beats. A doorbell rings. MR BRAUN gets up and exits. Muffled voices are heard offstage. MR BRAUN re-enters, followed by CHAD. CHAD wears a coat, gloves, boots, and a stocking cap. CHAD holds a paper plate of Christmas cookies wrapped in clear plastic.)

(A beat)

CHAD: Hey, Jeff.

MR BRAUN: Chad came over with a plate of cookies for us.

CHAD: Merry Christmas.

MR BRAUN: Are you having a nice Christmas, Chad?

CHAD: We already opened our presents.

MR BRAUN: I hope you got something you liked.

CHAD: Yeah.

MR BRAUN: We were just opening our presents.

JEFF: I'll be right back. *(He exits.)*

MR BRAUN: What did you get?

CHAD: A sweater.

MR BRAUN: I got a new belt.

CHAD: Me too.

MR BRAUN: Hm.

CHAD: It was in my stocking.

(The Christmas music is suddenly turned off.)

(A beat. JEFF *re-enters. He has a plate of cookies that looks a lot like the one* CHAD *brought, except* JEFF's *is wrapped in green cellophane.)*

MR BRAUN: Here's a plate of cookies for your family. Jeff and I made those. Here. Jeff?

*(*JEFF *unwraps the green cellophane and begins to eat the cookies.)*

MR BRAUN: Oh.

CHAD: My mom just wanted me to stop by with some cookies for your family.

MR BRAUN: Tell your mom, "thank you".

CHAD: Okay.

MR BRAUN: Did you need a ride back home?

CHAD: No. I walked.

MR BRAUN: That's too far of a walk. Let me give you a ride back.

CHAD: That's okay.

MR BRAUN: I'll drop you off on my way to the nursing home. You remember Matt's grandma, Grandma Fander?

CHAD: Yes.

MR BRAUN: When was the last time you saw her?

CHAD: With Matt.

MR BRAUN: You guys were visiting her?

CHAD: Our music class was doing a holiday play at the nursing home and she was there.

MR BRAUN: You were doing a Christmas play?

CHAD: A holiday play.

MR BRAUN: Wow. Maybe we could stop at the nursing home first so that you could say "hi" to her. We need to make a quick stop and take some presents over there. Maybe you can do some of your Christmas play for her?

JEFF: We're taking Chad to the nursing home with us?

MR BRAUN: It's on the way.

JEFF: You could have gone last night.

MR BRAUN: I was at church.

CHAD: I wouldn't mind seeing her.

MR BRAUN: Great!

(*A beat.* MR BRAUN *exits.* JEFF *and* CHAD *look at each other.* MR BRAUN *re-enters with a huge, plastic garbage bag and begins to stuff it full of the paper and boxes that are scattered on the floor.*)

(*Lights fade.*)

Scene 5

(MRS BRAUN *sits in her jail cell.*)

MRS BRAUN: Right after my father died, I could smell electric shave. Also, my cousin had a strange thing happen to him. When he was young, he had this habit of climbing one of my father's peach trees, and eating peaches from its branches. Whenever my father would catch him, he would always say, "Kevin, get out of that tree!", then my father would whistle real loud. Kevin would always climb from the tree and run all the way home. About two weeks after my father died, my cousin was still into the habit of climbing that peach tree and eating peaches in the branches. He was sitting on a branch in the middle of the day eating a peach when he heard, "Kevin, get out of that tree!" and that same loud whistle. Kevin was so scared he fell out of the tree and nearly broke his leg, and almost choked to death on a peach. Only recently, about three years ago, did Kevin tell me that story. He says it still frightens him to think about it.

(Lights fade.)

Scene 6

(MR BRAUN, JEFF, GRANDMA *and* CHAD *sit at a table at the nursing home. They all have a plastic glass in front of them, which is filled with egg-nog.* GRANDMA *wears a wrinkled sweat suit.* MR BRAUN *has three gifts in a large, paper bag.)*

MR BRAUN: Merry Christmas, Margaret.

JEFF: Merry Christmas.

CHAD: Merry Christmas.

MR BRAUN: Hey, Margaret. We brought you the rest of your presents. *(He takes the presents from the bag.)* This one's from Steve and Shelly, and this one's from us, and this one's from Steve and Shelly, too.

GRANDMA: No, she was going to leave and she didn't want it. No, she didn't shucka shucka shucka shucka—

MR BRAUN: Uh-huh.

(GRANDMA *smoothes out the wrapping paper on the presents.)*

MR BRAUN: Do you want to open the presents? *(He takes* GRANDMA's *hand.)* Here. Tear here. It's already started.

JEFF: Dad, did you see what Joel got her?

MR BRAUN: No.

JEFF: He got her a music box. It's got some strange angel on top of it.

MR BRAUN: An angel?

JEFF: When you wind it up it plays the song *Memory* from *Cats*

MR BRAUN: It does?

JEFF: Yes.

MR BRAUN: I'm sure they didn't mean anything. *(Pause)* It has glass on it?

JEFF: I guess.

MR BRAUN: She really can't have that in her room.

(GRANDMA *points at, then touches* CHAD's *face.* CHAD *is startled.* MR BRAUN *moves* GRANDMA's *hands from* CHAD's *face.*)

GRANDMA: She didn't know, you see, something better was something better... *(Clicking sounds)*—

MR BRAUN: We should open her other presents. *(He unwraps one of the presents. It's a sweatshirt. The sweatshirt is like the one she is wearing, but new.)* That's a nice sweatshirt. Who's that from, again?

(MR BRAUN *shows the sweatshirt to* GRANDMA. *She smoothes the sweatshirt out on the table.*)

MR BRAUN: Where's our present?

JEFF: Here. *(He opens her present. The present is some slippers.)* Slippers.

(GRANDMA *picks up her egg-nog and begins to drink it.*)

MR BRAUN: I hope we got the right size.

(JEFF *opens her other present.*)

JEFF: Sweat bottoms.

MR BRAUN: They go with the top. Here, Margaret. See?

(MR BRAUN *shows her the sweat bottoms.* GRANDMA *finishes her egg-nog.)*

MR BRAUN: She really likes egg-nog. *(He laughs.)*

JEFF: Have mine, grandma.

MR BRAUN: She doesn't need more egg-nog.

JEFF: She wants more.

(GRANDMA *begins to drink* JEFF's *egg-nog.)*

MR BRAUN: *(To* CHAD*)* She's probably a little different than the last time you were here.

CHAD: Yeah.

MR BRAUN: We should get you home, Chad.

(MR BRAUN *cleans up all the wrapping paper and exits with the loose pile.)*

GRANDMA: Yes, yes, yes, yes.

(GRANDMA *touches* CHAD's *face again.* CHAD *does not move. He sits still, staring at* JEFF.*)*

(A few beats)

(MR BRAUN *re-enters and moves* GRANDMA's *hand from* CHAD's *face.)*

MR BRAUN: Everybody ready?

JEFF: I'll take her back to her room.

(JEFF *helps* GRANDMA *out of her chair.* JEFF *and* GRANDMA *exit.)*

MR BRAUN: When do you go back to school, Chad?

CHAD: Soon.

MR BRAUN: What date do you go back?

CHAD: January 6th.

MR BRAUN: That's still a long ways away.

CHAD: They give us two and a half weeks.

MR BRAUN: Your folks probably think you got lost with those cookies.

CHAD: Yeah.

(Lights fade.)

Scene 7

(GRANDMA sits. She has a blanket over her.)

GRANDMA: And there she was, there she was. We were all there and there she was. I tried to see her, but no. No no no. *(Long pause)* We went up, you see, we went up, and she wasn't there. I wanted to see her, but she wasn't there. No, she wasn't there. That's what she wasn't there no no. We were all there, she wasn't going to go. She told them she wasn't going to go, and she she she was going, no no no. Shucka shucka shucka shucka shucka... It's the *(Muffled sounds)*, it's the... He didn't know, he didn't know. She was down, down. I didn't tell them. I didn't tell them any of what they were saying. That's not what she wanted. No, no. She didn't want it, she left then. It was out of the window, you could see the flowers. They were there, and then down the driveway. You could see the yellow flowers then down the driveway. She was there, and she saw flowers. I wanted to get flowers, I wanted to get them but she wasn't there. I'd like to go, I'd like to go out there. Yes? I'd like to go out there and see it. I'd like to see it. She was laughing, she was laughing and then yes yes, then she was going. No, no...

(GRANDMA carefully stands, then exits very slowly.)

(Lights fade.)

Scene 8

(CHAD *and* MR BRAUN *sit at a fast food restaurant. They both have bags of fast food in front of them, as well as sodas.*)

MR BRAUN: I can't believe they're open.

CHAD: Yeah.

MR BRAUN: I can't usually eat this, but today it's Christmas so I don't care.

CHAD: Oh.

MR BRAUN: It usually messes up my stomach.

CHAD: Thanks for lunch.

MR BRAUN: Thanks for letting me drive all the way out to the courthouse so that I could drop Jeff off.

CHAD: Are you going to visit Matt at the cemetery today?

MR BRAUN: When Mrs Braun gets home. We forgot to do some of your holiday play at the nursing home.

CHAD: That's okay.

MR BRAUN: That was for music class?

CHAD: Yes. In fifth grade.

MR BRAUN: What part did Matt play?

CHAD: He was a present.

MR BRAUN: I don't think I got to see it.

CHAD: He was a big present.

MR BRAUN: A big present?

CHAD: There were five or six big presents in the play. The people that were presents all wore big cardboard boxes that were wrapped with gift wrap. Their heads stuck out of the top, and their arms came out of the sides. They had bows on top of their heads.

MR BRAUN: Oh.

CHAD: I played the judge. I wore a judge's robe.

(CHAD *and* MR BRAUN *quietly open their bags, unwrap their food, and begin to eat.*)

MR BRAUN: Did you know that Mrs Braun had gotten in trouble?

CHAD: Yes.

MR BRAUN: Did you see her in the newspaper?

CHAD: Yes.

MR BRAUN: The whole thing really wasn't as bad as the article made it sound.

CHAD: I just saw the picture of her.

MR BRAUN: It was a bad picture.

CHAD: Oh.

MR BRAUN: Did you want some ketchup?

(CHAD *pulls about fifteen packets of ketchup from his bag.* MR BRAUN *laughs hard.*)

(*Pause*)

MR BRAUN: I really don't eat here often. My stomach.

CHAD: I used to come here with my parents.

MR BRAUN: I haven't been here in years.

CHAD: We used to come here for lunch after church.

MR BRAUN: You did?

CHAD: I guess not every time.

MR BRAUN: Jeff is picking up Mrs Braun's car at the station house.

CHAD: Oh.

MR BRAUN: They impounded her car along with the other folk's cars that were outside. The people she was with had parked their cars a couple of blocks away because they were ordered not to come within thirty feet of the clinic or the doctor or any of the women. Then they just walked over there anyway and stood blocking the entrance. Afterwards, the police got the license numbers of the cars and impounded them. Jeff is going to pick her up so that she doesn't have to drive herself. They should be back when I get home.

CHAD: That's good.

MR BRAUN: She has had a tough time. They offered her a chance to come home earlier, but she told them she wanted to carry out her sentence. During the arrest, the newspaper took that picture of her and then they wrote that article. Even though the article only mentioned her name one time, that picture made it look like the whole thing was about her. Mrs Braun believes very strongly in what she is doing, and there have been a lot of people calling to tell me they're praying for her.

CHAD: Good.

MR BRAUN: A lot of people have told me that they can understand and see her point of view.

CHAD: I can understand her point of view.

MR BRAUN: You can?

CHAD: I guess I can.

MR BRAUN: I can, too. (Pause) How is school going?

CHAD: Fine.

MR BRAUN: You're in high school next year.

CHAD: Yeah.

MR BRAUN: Are you ready? You'll be a freshman.

CHAD: I guess I'm ready.

MR BRAUN: It'll be pretty different at the high school.

CHAD: It shouldn't be that bad.

MR BRAUN: No.

CHAD: I'm looking forward to it.

MR BRAUN: The science classes will be harder. But maybe you can do a science project, like you and Matt did. Maybe you can be in the science fair. You and Matt had a great science fair project.

CHAD: It wasn't very good.

MR BRAUN: You and Matt showed how blood flows in the body by using celery stalks. You guys had a microscope set up and had magnified a vein from the celery.

CHAD: It wasn't a very good project.

MR BRAUN: You guys worked hard on it.

CHAD: We got a C-minus.

MR BRAUN: You did?

CHAD: Yes.

MR BRAUN: I don't remember what grade you and Matt got.

CHAD: We got a C-minus.

MR BRAUN: I remember you and Matt doing the blood flow project for the science fair.

CHAD: Marci Ringer's project won. She got an A.

MR BRAUN: I don't remember that. What else happened at the science fair?

CHAD: Nothing, really.

MR BRAUN: Did you guys have fun?

CHAD: Yes.

MR BRAUN: I can't believe you guys got a C-minus.

CHAD: I know. Oh well.

(Pause. CHAD *and* MR BRAUN *eat.)*

(Lights fade.)

Scene 9

(Lights up on MRS BRAUN. *She is in a waiting area of the jail.)*

MRS BRAUN: I've seen a picture of a ghost. The name of the ghost is "The Brown Lady". The picture was probably taken in the 1920's or the 1930's, and it's of a long staircase. In the picture, you can see wooden stairs with a center runner, and at the bottom you can see the end of the stair's railing. In the center of the picture is a form of some kind. The form is white and transparent and floats just above the ground, as if it were floating down the steps.

*(*JEFF *enters quietly behind* MRS BRAUN. *She does not notice come in.)*

MRS BRAUN: The form clearly has the shape of a woman. If you look closely, you can see her face and arms, but her bottom half fades down into the steps. I don't know the history of "The Brown Lady", or where the picture was taken, but the photo has been examined by experts. No one doubts that it is a true picture of a ghost. And the ghost is beautiful. She was once a very beautiful woman who had walked down this long, dark stairway. She is graceful and elegant. "The Brown Lady" walks down that stairway eternally, living and moving forever.

JEFF: Merry Christmas, Mom.

MRS BRAUN: *(Pause)* Jeff. Did you get the car?

JEFF: You have to sign for it at the lot.

MRS BRAUN: Did they give you the keys?

JEFF: Yes.

MRS BRAUN: I'm ready, then.

(MRS BRAUN exits. A pause. JEFF exits.)

(Lights fade.)

Scene 10

(MR BRAUN and CHAD sit at the Braun home. CHAD is eating a sugar cookie.)

MR BRAUN: They should be home any minute now.

CHAD: Great.

MR BRAUN: I know that Mrs Braun would like very much to say "hi" to you, and thank you for the plate of cookies you brought over. It'll just be a few minutes then I'll drive you on home.

CHAD: It would be nice to see her.

MR BRAUN: She'll be happy to be home.

CHAD: Yeah.

MR BRAUN: Chad?

CHAD: Yeah?

MR BRAUN: Do you want another cookie?

CHAD: That's okay.

MR BRAUN: You can have some of the ones you brought.

CHAD: We have lots still at home.

MR BRAUN: Cookies are good. *(Long pause)* When did you and Matt do that science fair project?

CHAD: It was seventh grade science class. It was the first semester of last year.

MR BRAUN: You guys were lab partners?

CHAD: Mister Polastrini split the class up using opposite ends of the alphabet.

MR BRAUN: What was your teacher's name?

CHAD: Mister Polastrini.

MR BRAUN: Last year. Seventh grade.

CHAD: The first semester of seventh grade.

MR BRAUN: It seemed like you were lab partners for longer than that.

CHAD: Mister Polastrini's class was hard.

MR BRAUN: It was?

CHAD: He made us dissect things. Most people don't have to dissect anything until eighth grade.

MR BRAUN: Oh.

CHAD: We had lab assignments and everything.

MR BRAUN: That seems early to be dissecting.

CHAD: Mister Polastrini wanted to see if we could do it.

MR BRAUN: You and Matt dissected things together?

CHAD: If you were in the class, you had to dissect or you would get an "F".

MR BRAUN: I don't remember him saying he had to do that.

CHAD: We dissected a worm, a frog and a goldfish.

MR BRAUN: You guys dissected all of those?

CHAD: Yes.

MR BRAUN: Did you like it?

CHAD: This year we dissected a fetal pig.

MR BRAUN: Jeff dissected a fetal pig in eighth grade.

CHAD: Hm.

MR BRAUN: I remember he said that he had to be very careful not to cut the pig's veins or arteries because they had to examine them separately later for the lab assignment.

CHAD: We didn't have to do that.

MR BRAUN: Matt would have liked to dissect a fetal pig.

CHAD: My lab partner ate part of the ear off of his pig.

(Pause)

MR BRAUN: You should probably get home.

CHAD: It's okay. I don't mind waiting to say "hi" to Mrs Braun.

MR BRAUN: Maybe her car wouldn't start. It's been sitting in that lot for awhile.

CHAD: I don't mind waiting.

MR BRAUN: Maybe I should drive back over there. They might need a ride.

CHAD: Maybe.

MR BRAUN: I hope the car didn't conk out on their way back. Ah, I'm sure they're fine.

CHAD: Yeah.

MR BRAUN: You want to wait?

CHAD: I don't mind.

(A beat. Lights fade.)

Scene 11

(MRS BRAUN *and* JEFF *are with* GRANDMA *in the nursing home.* GRANDMA *wanders as* MRS BRAUN *attempts to have her sit in a chair.)*

MRS BRAUN: Why don't you sit.

GRANDMA: I told her that was shucka shucka shucka—

MRS BRAUN: Sit, Mom. Just sit down right here so we can talk.

(MRS BRAUN *puts* GRANDMA *sitting into the chair.)*

MRS BRAUN: *(To* JEFF*)* Where is the music box?

JEFF: It's not really a music box. There's no box part.

MRS BRAUN: She can't have something like that in here. It could break.

JEFF: I put it in her room in a drawer.

MRS BRAUN: I don't know why Joel sent that to her. He knows mom can't have something like that here.

JEFF: It plays *Memory* from *Cats.*

MRS BRAUN: I'm sure that was a mistake. They probably didn't listen to it first.

JEFF: Steve and Shelly got her a sweatshirt.

MRS BRAUN: Good.

(GRANDMA *stands and begins to walk away from her chair.)*

MRS BRAUN: Mom, sit so we can talk.

JEFF: Dad's home by now, after he dropped Chad Udelhoven off.

MRS BRAUN: That was nice of the Udelhovens to bring over those cookies. *(To* GRANDMA*)* Mom, sit.

JEFF: Who were you talking to?

MRS BRAUN: When?

JEFF: When I came in to get you at the courthouse.

MRS BRAUN: I wasn't talking to anyone.

JEFF: Yes you were.

MRS BRAUN: It's none of your business.

JEFF: What do you mean?

MRS BRAUN: It's none of your business.

JEFF: Why not?

MRS BRAUN: Jeff. I want to spend some time with my mother on Christmas.

JEFF: Go ahead.

MRS BRAUN: Go and get that music box for me out of her room.

(JEFF *exits.* MRS BRAUN *walks to* GRANDMA *and helps her into the chair again.*)

MRS BRAUN: There you go, mom.

GRANDMA: She was here and then she went down down and I was here I don't and then she was laughing laughing, and then she was gone and then she left and was going and and here I was here she was laughing I was and I didn't know yeah yeah—

MRS BRAUN: She was laughing?

(MRS BRAUN *sits with* GRANDMA.)

(*Pause*)

(JEFF *enters, holding the music box.*)

JEFF: Here.

(JEFF *hands* MRS BRAUN *the music box. A pause*)

MRS BRAUN: Oh boy! *(Laughs hard)*

JEFF: Look.

(JEFF winds up the music box. The angel spins while playing the song "Memory" from the musical "Cats". MRS BRAUN continues to laugh.)

(MRS BRAUN slowly stops laughing.)

(Lights fade.)

Scene 12

(The BRAUN house. CHAD sits in the same chair he was sitting in previously. A few beats. MR BRAUN enters quickly with a large, cardboard box.)

MR BRAUN: Here it is. It should be in here. *(He begins to look in the box. It is filled with notebook papers and folders.)* He sure had a lot of school work.

CHAD: Yeah.

MR BRAUN: More work than I remember having when I was in school.

CHAD: Yeah.

MR BRAUN: Jeff didn't have this much. This is too much. *(He again rummages through the box.)* Here it is. *(He pulls out a red folder. Reading)* "Earth Science". *(He opens the folder and looks through it.)* I don't see it. What was the name of the project?

CHAD: I don't remember what we named it.

(MR BRAUN pulls something from the folder.)

MR BRAUN: What's this? *(He looks carefully at a piece of notebook paper. There are small drawings on the paper of stick men in a battle. He holds it up for CHAD to see.)* Is this Matt's?

CHAD: Probably.

MR BRAUN: He drew this? What is it?

CHAD: He was just drawing war. Lots of guys in seventh grade used to draw war.

MR BRAUN: Is this blood?

CHAD: We had red pens for science class, so the ones anyone drew in science had a lot of blood.

MR BRAUN: These people are all broken apart.

CHAD: Sometimes you would start one and the other guy would finish it.

MR BRAUN: This is Matt's?

CHAD: Nobody draws those anymore.

MR BRAUN: He drew these people?

CHAD: They're stick men. *(Pause)* Lots of guys drew war.

MR BRAUN: The drawings all looked like this?

CHAD: Mostly.

MR BRAUN: This is his?

CHAD: Probably.

(A beat)

(MR BRAUN closes the box, and exits with it.)

(Pause)

(MR BRAUN enters without the box. He sits. A beat)

MR BRAUN: I should get you back home.

CHAD: I don't mind waiting.

MR BRAUN: Maybe we'll see them on the way. We can look for them as we go.

CHAD: That's okay.

MR BRAUN: I'll drive for awhile and if we see her we'll stop. If we don't then I'll drive you on home.

CHAD: Okay.

MR BRAUN: The roads shouldn't be too slick.

(Lights fade.)

Scene 13

(JEFF and MRS BRAUN at the fast food restaurant. They sit eating some fast food.)

MRS BRAUN: I'm surprised they're open on Christmas.

JEFF: Me too.

MRS BRAUN: We should probably hurry so we can all go to the cemetery later. I just was getting the shakes from being so hungry. *(Pause)* When does school start again?

JEFF: January 10th.

MRS BRAUN: That's a ways away.

JEFF: I guess.

MRS BRAUN: They give you quite a break.

JEFF: Yeah.

MRS BRAUN: Did Mrs Kenworthy call?

JEFF: Yes.

MRS BRAUN: She was setting up the next event.

JEFF: She called with the information, but I told her you'd call her back.

MRS BRAUN: Good.

JEFF: You've got her phone number so I didn't write it down.

MRS BRAUN: I'm doing this for the children, Jeff.

JEFF: I know.

MRS BRAUN: I don't want you to worry.

JEFF: I'm not worried.

MRS BRAUN: That's good.

JEFF: Dad got me a sweatshirt.

MRS BRAUN: I'll have to take care of Christmas this week. What did you get your dad for Christmas?

JEFF: I got him a C D.

MRS BRAUN: Did he listen to it yet?

JEFF: I don't know.

MRS BRAUN: I'm sure he'll like it.

JEFF: Yeah.

MRS BRAUN: I'm done eating.

JEFF: Okay.

MRS BRAUN: Are you almost finished?

JEFF: Almost.

MRS BRAUN: Are you doing anything interesting in school?

JEFF: I did okay on my finals.

MRS BRAUN: That's great.

(Pause. MRS BRAUN *stands and puts her coat on, then sits back in her chair.)*

*(*JEFF *eats semi-quickly.)*

(Lights fade.)

Scene 14

(CHAD *and* MR BRAUN *are at a cemetery, standing in front of a small, snow covered grave. The grave is inserted into the ground, and looks more like an enlarged marble plaque than a headstone.)*

MR BRAUN: I was going to stop later. I was waiting for Mrs Braun and we were all going to stop together for Christmas.

CHAD: I haven't been here since Matt's funeral.

MR BRAUN: It was on the way. I'll run you home afterwards.

CHAD: Okay.

MR BRAUN: I haven't been here in awhile.

(They stand in silence for a few beats.)

MR BRAUN: I'll come back later. Are you ready, Chad?

CHAD: No.

MR BRAUN: I should probably get you back home.

CHAD: I have to tell you something, Mister Braun.

MR BRAUN: You do?

CHAD: Yes.

MR BRAUN: What is it?

CHAD: I feel really bad.

MR BRAUN: What is it?

CHAD: I feel so bad about it.

MR BRAUN: Can you tell me in the car?

CHAD: About six months before Matt died I was at this party over at Amy Hartman's house and Matt was

there. It was in the basement of her house and mostly
we just stood around and ate. Later, we decided to play
light as a feather. Matt was the person who was dead so
we turned off the lights and he laid down on the floor.
The floor was concrete and it was really cold, I don't
know how he just laid there. We all put our fingers
under Matt and then someone started the story about
how Matt had become dead. It was about a car accident
and at the beginning people were goofing around and
laughing and then as the story went on and it was so
dark and all you could do was hear the people talking
and Matt breathing real low and each of us spoke.
The story went around the circle twice and then we
got to the end and Matt was dead. So we all said that
he was as light as a feather three times, he's as light
as a feather, he's as light as a feather, he's as light as a
feather, and we all picked him up with our fingers and
he was. He was as light as a feather and we all picked
him up into the air. We were holding him in the air for
awhile. He was as light as a feather. Then we put him
down. It was really silent. It was really cold.

MR BRAUN: Do you think that game has something to
do with Matt's death?

CHAD: I don't know.

MR BRAUN: You've got to be stupid.

CHAD: I thought God was watching us.

MR BRAUN: Are you stupid?

CHAD: I don't know.

MR BRAUN: Matt's death was an accident. You must be
stupid to think that this crap had anything to do with
Matt's death. Matt was accidentally shot in the head,
Chad.

CHAD: I know.

MR BRAUN: It was a goddamn accident.

CHAD: I know.

MR BRAUN: I've got to get home.

CHAD: No.

MR BRAUN: Let's go.

CHAD: I feel so bad!

MR BRAUN: Come on, or I'm leaving you!

CHAD: I just wanted to tell you! I knew you'd be upset!

MR BRAUN: Some stupid party game didn't do anything to Matt.

CHAD: I'm so sorry, Mister Braun!

MR BRAUN: It was a goddamn accident, Chad! *(He exits.)*

(Pause. CHAD sits on the ground near the grave.)

(Lights fade.)

END ACT ONE

ACT TWO

Scene 1

(The BRAUN's *home.* MRS BRAUN *sits in a chair, with a Christmas present on her lap.* MR BRAUN *stands next to* MRS BRAUN's *chair.* JEFF *sits in the other chair.)*

MRS BRAUN: This is a present from Tom.

*(*MRS BRAUN *unwraps the present. It's a bath pillow.)*

*(*JEFF *quickly takes a photo.)*

MRS BRAUN: This will be nice.

*(*MRS BRAUN *hands the pillow to* JEFF.)*

JEFF: A bath pillow.

MRS BRAUN: That should be nice in the tub. It has terry cloth on it. It's from Tom.

*(*JEFF *attempts to hand the pillow to* MR BRAUN. MR BRAUN *doesn't notice.* JEFF *nudges* MR BRAUN.)*

MR BRAUN: Oh.

JEFF: Here.

*(*JEFF *hands the pillow to* MR BRAUN.)*

MR BRAUN: This is nice.

MRS BRAUN: I like it. *(Pause)* Are there any more presents?

JEFF: No.

MRS BRAUN: Okay. *(Pause)* I would really like all of us to go out to the nursing home, then we should go to the cemetery afterwards.

JEFF: I've already been to the nursing home twice today.

MRS BRAUN: I think we should all go together.

JEFF: Dad and I went this morning.

MRS BRAUN: I know.

JEFF: We already gave her her presents.

MRS BRAUN: I just thought it would be good if all of us went to see her.

MR BRAUN: You two go ahead. I need to do a few things around here.

MRS BRAUN: I want the three of us to go.

MR BRAUN: I've already been to the nursing home today.

JEFF: *(To* MRS BRAUN*)* Don't you want to stay home for awhile?

MRS BRAUN: Yes, but it wouldn't take a long time just to go out to see mom.

MR BRAUN: We don't have to run around all day.

MRS BRAUN: I'm not running around.

MR BRAUN: I have to put gas in my car.

MRS BRAUN: That's fine. Jeff and I will take my car and meet you at the nursing home in the lobby. Then we can all see her together.

(Pause)

MR BRAUN: I'll get my coat.

MRS BRAUN: This will be nice for mom.

JEFF: I was just at the nursing home.

(Lights fade.)

Scene 2

(The nursing home. GRANDMA *sits, looking worn.* CHAD *sits next to her with his coat on. He shivers slightly.)*

GRANDMA: He didn't know, he didn't know. She was down, down. I didn't tell them. I didn't tell them any of what they were saying. Yes, yes. Shucka shucka shucka... Yes? Yes?

*(*CHAD *tries to put* GRANDMA's *hand on his face, but* GRANDMA *lets it drop to the table.)*

GRANDMA: Oh no. That's not what she wanted. She was going she was going. She said that no one was going to tell her, and then she didn't come. She didn't want to do that. No, no. She didn't want it. I'd like to go, I'd like to go out there. Yes? I'd like to go out there and see it. I'd like to see it.

*(*GRANDMA *smooths out a wrinkle in* CHAD's *coat.)*

(A few beats.)

*(*JEFF, MRS BRAUN *and* MR BRAUN *enter. They all are wearing coats.)*

MRS BRAUN: Hello?

JEFF: Chad?

MRS BRAUN: Chad Udelhoven? What are you doing here?

MR BRAUN: Hello.

MRS BRAUN: What happened? Are you okay?

JEFF: Chad? What are you doing?

MR BRAUN: Let me get you home.

CHAD: *(To* MR BRAUN*)* I'm sorry.

MR BRAUN: Let's go.

MRS BRAUN: Why are you sorry?

CHAD: *(To* MR BRAUN*)* I didn't mean to make you mad.

JEFF: What are you doing here?

CHAD: I got cold.

JEFF: You got cold?

MRS BRAUN: *(To* MR BRAUN*)* Why don't you drive him home.

MR BRAUN: Okay.

JEFF: I can drive him.

MRS BRAUN: You shouldn't stay outside and get so cold, Chad.

JEFF: Let's go, Chad. I'll drive you home.

MR BRAUN: I'll drive him.

MRS BRAUN: Let Jeff do it.

MR BRAUN: Okay.

JEFF: Let's go, Chad.

CHAD: Goodbye, Mrs Fander.

(GRANDMA *stares at* CHAD. GRANDMA *tries to stand.)*

MRS BRAUN: No, Mom, you sit.

MR BRAUN: Goodbye, Chad.

MRS BRAUN: It was nice to see you. Tell your mother thank you for the cookie plate.

CHAD: Bye.

JEFF: I'll take mom's car, then I'll meet you back at home.

MRS BRAUN: Okay.

(CHAD *and* JEFF *exit.)*

(Pause)

MRS BRAUN: Hi Mom. Merry Christmas.

(Lights fade.)

Scene 3

(CHAD and JEFF are at the fast food restaurant. JEFF is eating. CHAD sucks on a straw attached to a pop.)

JEFF: Do you want some fries?

CHAD: No.

JEFF: I'll buy.

CHAD: No, thank you.

JEFF: Are you okay?

CHAD: Yes.

JEFF: Why were you at the nursing home?

CHAD: It was close and I was cold.

JEFF: Close to where?

CHAD: Nowhere.

JEFF: Did my dad drop you off at your house before?

CHAD: Yes.

JEFF: Bullshit.

CHAD: What?

JEFF: I said bullshit.

CHAD: I just was walking around after I went home.

JEFF: What did you do?

CHAD: Walked around.

JEFF: It's too cold to walk around.

CHAD: I know.

JEFF: Where did you go?

CHAD: I was just walking around.

JEFF: Listen, Chad. Tell me why the hell you were at the nursing home.

CHAD: I did tell you. I got cold so I went there.

JEFF: My dad didn't drop you off at your house, did he.

CHAD: I don't know.

JEFF: God damn tell me what happened or I'll beat the crap of you right here. He didn't drop you off at your house.

CHAD: *(Pause)* No, he didn't drop me off.

JEFF: Where did you go?

CHAD: To the cemetery to see Matt.

JEFF: You did?

CHAD: Yes.

JEFF: What did you do?

CHAD: Talked.

JEFF: About what?

CHAD: I told him something about Matt.

JEFF: What was it?

CHAD: That he played light as a feather.

JEFF: Oh.

CHAD: I should go home.

JEFF: Let me go get you some fries.

CHAD: That's okay.

JEFF: Then wait until I'm finished.

CHAD: Okay.

JEFF: Then he just left you out there in the cemetery?

CHAD: Yes.

JEFF: *(Pause)* Hm.

CHAD: I hadn't been there since Matt's funeral.

JEFF: Drink your pop.

(CHAD drinks his pop.)

(Lights fade.)

Scene 4

(MR BRAUN sits alone at the nursing home, looking at the piece of paper with Matt's drawing on it . The picture looks as if it has been folded up.)

(MRS BRAUN enters. MR BRAUN quickly puts the piece of paper away.)

MRS BRAUN: I can't find her new slippers. We gave them to her today and now they're gone already.

MR BRAUN: This place is nuts.

MRS BRAUN: Mom's room is so dark. I hate leaving her in there by herself. *(Pause)* I would like go out to the cemetery.

MR BRAUN: Okay.

MRS BRAUN: We need to pick up Jeff at home first.

MR BRAUN: Okay.

MRS BRAUN: It's nice to be out of prison.

(Pause)

(MR BRAUN slowly pulls Matt's drawing from his pocket. He unfolds it and looks at it for a moment.)

MR BRAUN: Have you ever seen this before?

(MR BRAUN *shows* MRS BRAUN *Matt's drawing.*)

MRS BRAUN: No.

MR BRAUN: It's a drawing of stick people having a war.

MRS BRAUN: Why are you showing me this?

MR BRAUN: I was looking through some of Matt's papers from school, his science class folder, and I found it. I asked Chad Udelhoven about it and he said Matt drew these things all the time.

MRS BRAUN: Boys draw pictures like that.

MR BRAUN: Not all of them.

MRS BRAUN: My brother used to draw pages of strange things.

MR BRAUN: These stick men are bleeding to death. There are pools of blood under them.

MRS BRAUN: You should put it back where you found it.

MR BRAUN: There are probably more of them in the folder.

MRS BRAUN: I'm ready to go.

MR BRAUN: There are tanks exploding and airplanes breaking apart. Men breaking in half, bleeding. Arms blown off of bodies.

MRS BRAUN: I'm ready to go.

MR BRAUN: Okay.

MRS BRAUN: I need to get mom some new slippers.

MR BRAUN: We can stop by the cemetery on the way back.

MRS BRAUN: I'd like to go home.

MR BRAUN: Okay.

MRS BRAUN: I want to stop somewhere and get some slippers so I can bring them by tomorrow morning.

MR BRAUN: It's Christmas. Everything's closed.

MRS BRAUN: I would like to enjoy the holiday.

MR BRAUN: I know.

MRS BRAUN: I want to go home now. We can go to the cemetery to see Matt later with Jeff. Later, the three of us can go together.

MR BRAUN: Okay.

(MRS BRAUN *exits.* MR BRAUN *folds the paper and puts it in his pocket.* MR BRAUN *exits.*)

(*Lights fade.*)

Scene 5

(JEFF *and* CHAD *are at the cemetery. They stand over Matt's grave.*)

JEFF: Hey. Your footprints.

CHAD: Yeah.

JEFF: And you were sitting right over here?

(JEFF *points to an area on the ground.*)

CHAD: Yeah.

(*Pause.* JEFF *sits where* CHAD *was sitting.*)

JEFF: (*To grave*) Hey, Matt.

CHAD: That's not funny.

JEFF: Are you kidding?

CHAD: I don't think that's very funny.

JEFF: You suddenly care?

CHAD: I just feel bad.

JEFF: Don't.

CHAD: He was a friend of mine.

JEFF: No he wasn't. He was your goddamn lab partner for one semester in seventh grade.

CHAD: We were also in a holiday play together.

JEFF: *(To* CHAD*)* Pussy.

CHAD: He was in my class.

JEFF: Shut-up.

(Long pause)

*(*JEFF *stands.* CHAD *is startled.)*

(Pause)

JEFF: You're scared of me.

CHAD: No I'm not.

JEFF: Yes.

CHAD: No.

JEFF: Everyone from Matt's grade is scared of me.

CHAD: I don't know.

JEFF: You are.

CHAD: I need to get home.

JEFF: You'll go home in a minute.

CHAD: I want to go.

(Pause)

JEFF: Did you know that Matt shot himself with my dad's gun?

CHAD: Yes.

JEFF: Did you know Matt died right in front of me?

CHAD: Those were in the newspaper.

JEFF: What kind of news is that?

CHAD: I don't know.

JEFF: That's not news. *(Pause)* How is eighth grade going?

CHAD: Fine.

JEFF: I remember eighth grade.

CHAD: It's not that bad.

JEFF: Wait until high school.

CHAD: I'm going to the car. *(Pause. He starts to walk away.)*

JEFF: Say bye to your best friend Matt.

(CHAD exits.)

JEFF: *(To grave)* Merry Christmas.

(Lights fade.)

Scene 6

(MR BRAUN and MRS BRAUN are at their home. They sit.)

MRS BRAUN: Ah, it's nice to be home.

MR BRAUN: I think I'm going to go for a walk.

MRS BRAUN: It's cold out there.

MR BRAUN: It's not too bad.

MRS BRAUN: Well, go ahead. It'll give me a chance to call Mrs Kenworthy and find out when the next event is.

MR BRAUN: You just got home.

MRS BRAUN: I'm not going anywhere. I'm just making a phone call.

MR BRAUN: I know.

MRS BRAUN: I want to tell her I'm home and I'm fine.

MR BRAUN: I know. *(Pause)* I understand your point of view.

MRS BRAUN: I'm doing this for the children.

MR BRAUN: I know.

MRS BRAUN: Go ahead on your walk. We can go to the cemetery later. Jeff should be home any minute.

MR BRAUN: Okay. *(He exits. A few beats. He enters wearing his coat, gloves, and hat.)* I'm going for a walk now.

MRS BRAUN: Okay. I might go out later.

MR BRAUN: Okay. I'll be right back after my walk.

MRS BRAUN: Okay.

(A beat. MR BRAUN exits towards the kitchen. He returns with a plate of cookies. MR BRAUN exits to go outside.)

(Lights fade.)

Scene 7

(CHAD's house. CHAD and JEFF sit near a small coffee table.)

JEFF: Do you have a pop?

(CHAD exits.)

(Pause)

(CHAD enters holding a pop.)

CHAD: Here.

JEFF: Thanks.

CHAD: I don't know where my parents went to. They should be home.

JEFF: Oh.

CHAD: They are probably at my aunt's.

JEFF: Did you get some good Christmas presents?

CHAD: Yes.

JEFF: What did you get?

CHAD: I don't know. A sweater.

JEFF: Hm. What else?

CHAD: A belt.

JEFF: My dad got a belt.

CHAD: It was an okay Christmas.

JEFF: Do you think my mom's crazy?

CHAD: No.

JEFF: You don't?

CHAD: No.

JEFF: She was in jail for a month.

CHAD: I know.

JEFF: She was talking to herself in jail.

CHAD: Hm.

JEFF: I walked in and she was talking about a ghost.

CHAD: I understand her point of view.

JEFF: What?

CHAD: I understand her point of view.

JEFF: What the hell does that mean?

CHAD: I just understand it.

JEFF: You do?

CHAD: Yes.

JEFF: What is it then?

CHAD: She cares about children.

JEFF: Who doesn't?

CHAD: She cares about other things.

JEFF: That's crap.

CHAD: I don't know.

JEFF: I think that my mom's crazy.

CHAD: Hm.

JEFF: I think that she misses Matt.

CHAD: She's Matt's mom.

JEFF: No kidding.

CHAD: I'm sorry I made your dad mad.

JEFF: You didn't make him mad.

CHAD: I told him—

JEFF: It doesn't matter what you told him.

CHAD: I'm sorry.

JEFF: I should hit you in the face or something.

CHAD: My parents should be right home.

JEFF: My mom was talking to the wall and she said it wasn't any of my business.

(Pause)

CHAD: I'm going to call over to my aunt's and see if my parents are there.

JEFF: Go ahead.

(Pause)

CHAD: I'll be right back.

(CHAD exits. JEFF drinks his pop.)

(Lights fade.)

Scene 8

(The nursing home. MRS BRAUN *sits with* GRANDMA.*)*

MRS BRAUN: This past summer I was sitting outside in our backyard and I saw what I thought was a squirrel. It was near evening, so I really didn't know what shadows belonged with what objects, when I noticed some movement near the top of the back fence. I really didn't pay that much attention to it. I relaxed my eyes for a moment, and when I opened them again, the shape had moved to the lawn. It also had seemed to grow slightly. I stood to look at it and noticed that it was vibrating. It was shaking like a hummingbird and gave off a dull buzzing sound. The sound grew as the shape's size grew until the it was about size of a small dog. I tried to go inside, but I couldn't. I was frozen staring at this spot, watching this thing grow. I realized I was watching something very strange. I was seeing something that was sent for me to see. I was experiencing this moment, this happening, and, Mom, something like a key entered me and turned, unlocking something. Then the shaking, buzzing thing on my lawn was gone. It had left nothing for me. Nothing had been unlocked, there had been no key. The shape was gone. It was getting dark, so I finished my dinner and went inside. Then it was nighttime.

(Pause)

GRANDMA: He didn't know, he didn't know. She was down, down. I didn't tell them. I didn't tell them any of what they were saying. Yes, yes. Shucka shucka shucka... Yes? Yes?

(Lights fade.)

Scene 9

(CHAD's *house.* CHAD *sits in a chair looking at a sweater and a belt.*)

(*There is knock at the door offstage.* CHAD *gets up and exits. A beat.* MR BRAUN, *holding a plate of cookies, enters.* CHAD *enters following.*)

MR BRAUN: I thought I should drop these off.

CHAD: Thanks.

MR BRAUN: I wanted to talk to you more.

CHAD: My parents should be home any minute. You can give them the cookies.

MR BRAUN: I want to know about Matt.

CHAD: I told you already.

MR BRAUN: I don't mean about what happened at some party. I want to know about him and his classes.

CHAD: The only classes I had with him were science and music.

MR BRAUN: Tell me about science class.

CHAD: I did already.

MR BRAUN: No, you didn't.

CHAD: I don't know what you want me to tell you about.

MR BRAUN: Tell me more about the class.

CHAD: It was hard.

MR BRAUN: What did you do?

CHAD: I told you.

MR BRAUN: Dissections. What else?

CHAD: We had to make a bug collection.

MR BRAUN: I remember that.

CHAD: We had to kill bugs and pin them to a board. One guy didn't kill his bugs all the way and they were flapping on his desk with pins stuck through them.

MR BRAUN: Matt was there?

CHAD: Yes.

MR BRAUN: What was the person's name who did that?

CHAD: It might have been Steve Cotton.

MR BRAUN: And you drew pictures of war in that class, too?

CHAD: Yes.

MR BRAUN: When?

CHAD: Before class started.

MR BRAUN: Tell me about Matt and these pictures.

CHAD: I already did.

MR BRAUN: Tell me more.

CHAD: I don't understand what you mean.

MR BRAUN: Why was he drawing these?

CHAD: I already told you. Everyone was drawing them.

MR BRAUN: Everyone in the class was doing this?

CHAD: Just the boys.

MR BRAUN: Did Matt say anything to you about the drawings?

CHAD: No.

MR BRAUN: What did you guys talk about?

CHAD: He said he was crazy.

MR BRAUN: He said he was what?

CHAD: He said he was crazy.

MR BRAUN: Why would he say that?

CHAD: He was joking.

MR BRAUN: What do you mean he was joking?

CHAD: I said he was weird and he said that he wasn't weird that he was crazy.

MR BRAUN: He wasn't weird.

CHAD: It was a joke. He was kidding.

MR BRAUN: Was everyone calling him weird?

CHAD: No. I don't know. There were other weird people in the class.

MR BRAUN: I'm not asking about other people.

CHAD: David Juvis stepped on a guppy in that class. That was weird.

MR BRAUN: I don't care about David Juvis!

CHAD: I know but I'm trying to tell you it was a joke!

MR BRAUN: Do you see that it's not?

CHAD: Matt was just kidding.

MR BRAUN: You shouldn't have been picking on Matt.

CHAD: I wasn't.

MR BRAUN: You guys did that project for the science fair and you went around calling him names.

CHAD: I didn't.

MR BRAUN: He wasn't crazy.

CHAD: I know.

MR BRAUN: You know, that was my gun that Matt shot himself with.

CHAD: I know.

MR BRAUN: I should tell your parents what you did to Matt.

CHAD: I didn't do anything.

MR BRAUN: You can't really tell me anything at all, can you?

CHAD: What do you want me to tell you?

MR BRAUN: This is unbelievable. I am really upset. *(Pause)* When did Jeff drop you off?

CHAD: He just left.

MR BRAUN: He just left now?

CHAD: Yes.

(Pause)

MR BRAUN: Tell your parents Merry Christmas.

(MR BRAUN exits. CHAD sits.)

(A long pause)

(A quick knocking is heard offstage. CHAD continues to sit. More knocks. CHAD remains seated.)

(JEFF enters.)

JEFF: What did my dad want?

CHAD: You can't just walk into someone's house.

JEFF: What was he telling you?

CHAD: My parents are on their way home and I really think you should go.

JEFF: After I left I saw my dad coming into your house.

CHAD: He wanted to drop off a plate of cookies.

JEFF: What did he say?

CHAD: He was dropping off cookies, see?

(CHAD points at the cookies. A beat.)

JEFF: Was he asking you about Matt?

CHAD: Yes.

JEFF: What did he want to know?

CHAD: Nothing.

JEFF: Tell me.

CHAD: He wanted to know what Matt did in school.

JEFF: When?

CHAD: In science class.

JEFF: Why?

(Pause. CHAD *sits silently.)*

JEFF: Chad?

CHAD: What.

JEFF: Do you want to know something about Matt?

CHAD: No.

JEFF: Something that nobody in your class, or anyone at school, knows?

CHAD: No.

JEFF: I'll tell you anyway.

CHAD: I don't want to know anything.

JEFF: I shot him.

CHAD: Please go home.

JEFF: Matt and I were home by ourselves playing war in the basement, and Matt had my dad's gun. We were playing for awhile, then we heard my mom upstairs opening the front door. We both started running around picking up stuff so it looked like we weren't doing anything and then I had the gun and I pointed it at Matt's head and I shot him and he fell over. My mom was at the top of the stairs and saw the whole

thing. Later, my mom told the police and my dad that
Matt had done it himself on accident so that no one
would think it was my fault, but it was. I shot Matt.

CHAD: I heard that story before.

JEFF: What?

CHAD: I had heard that story before.

JEFF: Where did you hear that?

CHAD: At school.

JEFF: You did?

CHAD: Someone told me that.

JEFF: It's the truth.

CHAD: I also heard that Matt killed himself.

JEFF: That's a lie.

CHAD: I heard that he put the gun in his mouth and
pulled the trigger.

JEFF: That's not true.

CHAD: I heard that at school.

JEFF: That's not true. The bullet went into Matt's head
and put a hole right there by his ear. Then the bullet
came out the other side of his head and made a huge
hole, and his brains and pieces of his skull went flying
all over the couch and the carpet and the wall. Blood
came out of his head and went all over and Matt's
mouth was hanging open and he fell down. When
he landed on the floor, more blood came out of his
head and more brains went all over the couch. He
was bleeding and my mom saw it happen and it was
my fault. I was the one that did it.

CHAD: That's a lie. You're lying. *(Long pause)* You
should go.

JEFF: Ask my mom if you don't believe me. *(Pause)* I'm not ready to go.

CHAD: Just go.

(A beat. JEFF exits.)

Scene 10

(MR BRAUN and JEFF are at the BRAUN home. Christmas music plays offstage.)

MR BRAUN: Are you hungry?

JEFF: Yes.

MR BRAUN: What should we have for dinner?

JEFF: I don't know.

MR BRAUN: I'll check the freezer and see what we have.

JEFF: I think there might be a pie in the freezer.

MR BRAUN: We should listen to that C D you got me for Christmas.

JEFF: Okay.

MR BRAUN: Your mother should be home any minute. *(Pause)* It was cold for Jesus's birthday today. But it didn't snow.

(Lights fade to black.)

END OF PLAY

www.ingramcontent.com/pod-product-compliance
Lightning Source LLC
Chambersburg PA
CBHW070030110426
42741CB00035B/2707